A Note to Parents

DK READERS is a compelling program for beginning readers, designed in conjunction with leading literacy experts, including Dr. Linda Gambrell, Professor of Education at Clemson University. Dr. Gambrell has served as President of the National Reading Conference and the College Reading Association, and has recently been elected to serve as President of the International Reading Association.

Beautiful illustrations and superb full-color photographs combine with engaging, easy-to-read text to offer a fresh approach to each subject in the series. Each DK READER is guaranteed to capture a child's interest while developing his or her reading skills, general knowledge, and love of reading.

The five levels of DK READERS are aimed at different reading abilities, enabling you to choose the books that are exactly right for your child:

Pre-level 1: Learning to read
Level 1: Beginning to read
Level 2: Beginning to read alone
Level 3: Reading alone
Level 4: Proficient readers

The "normal" age at which a child begins to read can be anywhere from three to eight years old, so these levels are only a general guideline.

No matter which level you select, you can be sure that you are helping your child learn to read, then read to learn!

LONDON, NEW YORK, MUNICH,
MELBOURNE, and DELHI

Senior Editor Catherine Saunders
Brand Manager Lisa Lanzarini
Publishing Manager Simon Beecroft
Category Publisher Siobhan Williamson
DTP Designer Santosh Kumar Ganapathula
Production Nick Seston
Reading Consultant
Linda Gambrell

Lucasfilm Ltd.
Executive Editor Jonathan Rinzler
Art Director Troy Alders
Continuity Editor Leland Chee
Director of Publishing Carol Roeder

First published in the United States in 2007 by
DK Publishing
375 Hudson Street
New York, New York 10014

10 11 10 9 8 7 6
SD298 – 05/07
Copyright © 2007 Lucasfilm Ltd and ™
Page design copyright © 2007 Dorling Kindersley Limited

DK Books are available at special discounts when
purchased in bulk for sales promotions, premiums,
fund-raising, or educational use.
For details, contact: DK Publishing Special Markets,
375 Hudson Street, New York, New York 10014
SpecialSales@dk.com

A catalog record for this book is available
from the Library of Congress.

ISBN: 978-0-7566-3112-3 (paperback)
ISBN: 978-0-7566-3113-0 (hardback)

Color reproduction by GRB Editrice S.r.l., London
Printed and bound by L-Rex, China.

starwars.com/fan

Discover more at
www.dk.com

Contents

DK READERS

LUCAS BOOKS

STAR WARS™
I WANT TO BE A
JEDI

READING **3** ALONE

Written by Simon Beecroft

DK

Mace Windu

Obi-Wan Kenobi

The Jedi

If you want to be a Jedi, you must learn all about Jedi ways. You must train hard. The Jedi are the best fighters in the galaxy, but their job is to keep the peace. A Jedi trains hard for many years. Then he or she travels around the galaxy to wherever there is trouble. The Jedi do all they can to bring peace without using violence.

A Jedi learns about a powerful energy field called the Force. The Force is everywhere. A Jedi must be able to understand and use the Force.

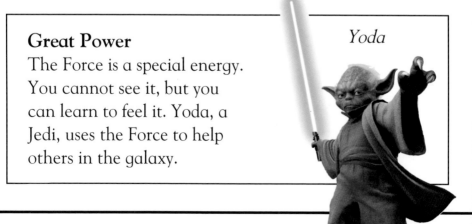

Yoda

Great Power
The Force is a special energy. You cannot see it, but you can learn to feel it. Yoda, a Jedi, uses the Force to help others in the galaxy.

Jedi usually go on missions in pairs.

Long Training

To be a Jedi, you must start your training when you are very young. First you will be a Youngling. If you pass the tests, you become a Padawan Learner. This means you are training to be a Jedi, but you are not a Jedi yet. If you train hard for several years and pass more tests, you will become a Jedi Knight.

When you are a Padawan you will
go on missions, but never alone. A more
experienced Jedi will always go with you.
A Jedi Master is the most experienced
Jedi of all. One day, if you continue to
learn and train, you too could become
a Jedi Master. Then you will train other,
younger Jedi apprentices. This is how
the Jedi Order works.

Spaceship
When you start to
go on missions, you
will fly in many kinds of
spaceships. This large ship usually
carries important politicians.

Special Powers

Jedi can come from anywhere in the galaxy. When they are very young, a boy or girl discovers that they have a special power. Perhaps they can move objects with their mind or they can do something really fast. They are using the Force without realizing it. This means that they could be a good Jedi.

One such person was Anakin Skywalker. Although he was very young, he was a great pilot. He flew a very fast machine called a Podracer and won a very dangerous race. A Jedi Master called Qui-Gon Jinn (pronounced KWY-GONN-JIN) met Anakin and decided to train him to be a Jedi. Qui-Gon Jinn thought that Anakin could become a great Jedi.

Anakin Skywalker is determined to win the Podrace.

Jedi in Training

When you begin training to be a Jedi you must leave your home and your parents. It's hard to leave behind everyone you love, so you must really want to be a Jedi. You travel from your home to a big planet at the center of the galaxy. A building called the Jedi Temple will be your home for the rest of your life. Here is where your Jedi training begins.

A New Home
The Jedi Temple is a gigantic building where all Jedi live, train, and work. It contains training halls, meeting rooms, libraries, and huge hangars for spaceships.

Using a training device, Jedi Master Yoda teaches the Younglings how to "see" without using their eyes.

At the Jedi Temple, you have many classes to learn all the Jedi skills. You learn to control your emotions so that you do not feel fear, anger, or hatred. You learn to use the Force. Sometimes, you will wear a special training helmet that covers your eyes. You will to learn to "see" only by using the Force.

Master and Learner

When you are training to be a Jedi,
you spend a lot of time with your teacher.
Your teacher will be a Jedi Master.
You will travel everywhere together.
You must always be prepared to learn
from your teacher.

Anakin Skywalker's teacher was called
Obi-Wan Kenobi (pronounced OH-BEE-
ONE KEN-OH-BEE). Anakin felt that
Obi-Wan was holding him back.

*Anakin does not always listen to what
Obi-Wan Kenobi tells him.*

*Anakin believes that Chancellor Palpatine is
a good man and listens to his advice.*

Anakin was impatient to become a
Jedi Knight. He was more powerful than
most Jedi, but he did not always obey the
rules of the Jedi Order. Anakin shared his
feelings of frustration with Chancellor
Palpatine (pronounced PAL-PA-TEEN).
Anakin thought that Palpatine was
a good friend to him.

Forbidden Marriage

Like everyone, the Jedi can fall in love, but they must not allow any strong emotions to get in the way of defending the galaxy. The Jedi are forbidden to marry because strong emotional attachments can cloud their judgment and stop them from doing their jobs well.

Anakin Skywalker knew that he was not allowed to get married, but he fell in love with a beautiful woman called Padmé Amidala (pronounced PAD-MAY AM-EE-DAL-AH). Anakin and Padmé secretly got married. If anyone found out that Anakin was married, he would have to stop being a Jedi.

The Jedi Council

The most powerful and wise Jedi sit
on the Jedi High Council. Their job is to
make all the most important decisions.
Twelve Jedi sit on the Council at any one
time. The Jedi Council meets in one of
the tall towers of the Jedi Temple. Two of
the most important members of the Jedi
Council are Yoda and Mace Windu.

Yoda is a very wise, green-skinned alien who is many hundreds of years old. Mace Windu is a human Jedi with great powers of thought. Yoda and Mace are both highly skilled with the Jedi's only weapon, which is called a lightsaber.

Mace Windu

Lightsabers

Lightsabers work like swords, but the blade is not made of metal. A lightsaber blade is made of glowing energy that can be many different colors. It is much more powerful than a metal blade, so a Jedi must learn how to use it safely and carefully. This is an important part of a Jedi's training.

Qui-Gon protects Queen Amidala from a battle droid.

Jedi must never use their lightsabers to attack others. They must use them only to defend and protect. Jedi are taught to respect life in any form.

Jedi build their own lightsabers, so every lightsaber is different. If you lose your lightsaber you must build another one yourself.

Lightsaber handle
You hold your lightsaber by the handle. When you activate it, the blade comes out of the end. The blade can slice through almost anything.

Lightsaber Combat

The Jedi use their lightsabers to defend themselves and others. Lightsabers can stop objects or deflect blaster fire. They can slice open sealed doors. Sometimes a Jedi has to fight someone else with a lightsaber. The Jedi use many fast moves to block their opponent. They use the Force to make their movements faster.

They also use the Force to guess what moves their opponent will make, even before they have made them.

Jedi Master Qui-Gon fights a deadly enemy named Darth Maul.

Mind Tricks

The Jedi can use the Force to influence the actions of other people. With a special wave of the hand, a Jedi can tell a person what he or she wants them to think or do. The person repeats back what the Jedi has just said, unaware that the Jedi has put the thought in their mind. This is called a Jedi mind trick.

Jedi mind tricks only work on certain people. They do not work on everyone. Certain strong-willed people can resist the Jedi mind trick.

All in the Mind
Once Obi-Wan used a Jedi mind trick on a small-time criminal. He convinced the crook to start living an honest life.

Anakin Skywalker used to be a slave owned by a flying alien called Watto. Qui-Gon tried to free Anakin by using a mind trick on Watto, but Watto could not be influenced.

Mind Powers

Jedi can also use the Force to move objects without touching them. For a Jedi, there is no difference between a large object and a small object. A skilled Jedi can move objects of any size—large or small.

Great Teacher
Yoda taught a young Jedi called Luke Skywalker
how to lift heavy objects using the Force. At first
Luke found it hard to believe it was possible.

Wise Jedi like Yoda can lift very heavy
objects using their mind alone. Yoda can
lift heavy rocks and even raise a spaceship
out of a swamp!

Jedi mind powers are also useful if a Jedi
drops his lightsaber in a battle. He can
quickly make it jump back into his hand
using the Force.

Jedi Equipment

The Jedi carry certain special tools when they go on a mission. They never know what they might need! They carry their tools on a special belt called a utility belt. They can hang their lightsaber on their utility belt. The belt also holds a medical kit, tools, food capsules, and a special communication device called a comlink. The Jedi use comlinks to send and receive messages.

Qui-Gon uses his comlink to speak with Obi-Wan Kenobi.

Comlink

Qui-Gon uses his holoprojector to show realistic pictures of a spaceship.

Another useful Jedi device is called a holoprojector, which enables a Jedi to record an image and then play it back later. A holoprojector can also transmit a moving image of yourself to someone else, like a video link.

Holoprojector

Special Missions

Special missions require special equipment. If you are going to swim underwater for long periods of time, you will need a Jedi breather. It fits into your mouth so you can breathe air through it. It holds enough air to last for two hours. Qui-Gon Jinn and Obi-Wan Kenobi once used breathers to reach an underwater city on the planet of Naboo.

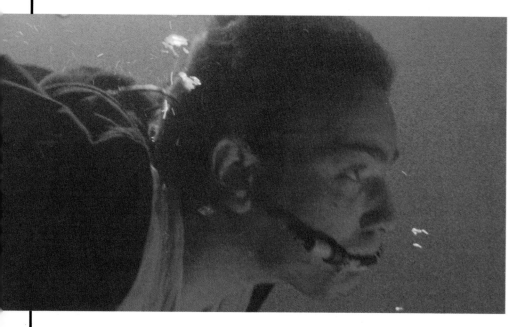

Another useful device is a pair of macrobinoculars. They electronically zoom in on objects that are very far away. They even work in the dark!

Tracer Beacon

If you want to keep track of a suspect, you could stick a tracer beacon to their spaceship. It sends signals that enable you to follow the spaceship.

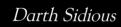

Darth Sidious

Deadly Enemies

The Jedi's deadly enemies are called the Sith. The first Sith were once Jedi, but they turned bad. Most Jedi use the Force for good but the Sith use the dark side of the Force to gain greater powers. The Sith want to destroy the Jedi.

A long time ago, the Sith and the Jedi fought a war. The Jedi defeated the Sith—or so they thought. Unknown to the Jedi, one Sith Master survived. The Sith Master secretly trained one other person so his skills would be passed on when he died. For a thousand years, each Sith Master trained one other person to keep the Sith skills alive. The final Sith Master was called Darth Sidious (pronounced SID-EE-US). He planned to destroy the Jedi once and for all.

Sith Battles

Sidious trained a ferocious alien called Maul. Maul had tattoos all over his head and horns on his skull. His teeth were razor sharp and his eyes were yellow. Maul fought with a deadly lightsaber with two blades, one at each end. He was a very fast fighter and the dark side of the Force gave him terrifying strength.

The Sith use lightsabers with red blades.

Sidious sent Maul to kill Qui-Gon and Obi-Wan. Maul killed Qui-Gon, but he was eventually defeated by Obi-Wan.

Dooku

When Maul was killed, Sidious had to find someone else to train. He found a Jedi Master called Dooku. Dooku had left the Jedi order and could not resist the chance to become a Sith.

Unusual Enemy

The Jedi and the Sith are usually
the only people who uses lightsabers.
However, the Sith Count Dooku trained
a man-droid to use a lightsaber.
His name was General Grievous
(pronounced GREE-VUS). General
Grievous fought with stolen lightsabers.
Each time he killed a Jedi in battle,
he took the Jedi's lightsaber.

Grievous was a deadly foe because his two mechanical arms could split into four. This meant he could fight with four lightsabers at the same time. During a war in the galaxy, Grievous fought Obi-Wan Kenobi. Grievous wanted to kill Obi-Wan and steal his lightsaber. The battle was ferocious, but in the end Obi-Wan managed to defeat Grievous.

War!

For thousands of years the Jedi were peacekeepers in the galaxy. The Jedi had no idea that the Sith were planning to destroy them. Anakin's friend Chancellor Palpatine was actually the Sith Lord Sidious. Sidious created huge armies of droids and started a war in the galaxy.

The first battle was on a dusty red planet called Geonosis (pronounced GEE-O-NO-SIS). The droid armies attacked the Jedi. Massive tanks on giant legs walked across the battlefield, firing all the time. Many Jedi were killed. Next, the droid armies began to attack planets, one after another.

Jedi Knight, Aayla Secura, goes into battle on a boggy world covered in giant fungus plants.

Brave Generals

When war began, the Jedi had to stop the droid armies from attacking every planet in the galaxy. There were far fewer Jedi in the galaxy than droid armies. Many Jedi became great generals. Yoda was commander of all the armies, with Mace alongside him.

The Jedi fought battles on many strange planets. Aayla Secura (pronounced AY-LA SEK-URE-RAH) went to a planet covered in dense jungles to stop an enemy attack. Ki-Adi-Mundi (pronounced KEE-ADDY-MUNDY) led an army to a dangerous enemy planet covered with crystals.

Ki-Adi-Mundi is a Jedi Master of great power and skill.

Jedi Pilots

The Jedi are some of the best pilots in the galaxy. Often they use their Force powers when they are flying spaceships.

Anakin Skywalker is one of the best pilots in the galaxy. He can fly at top speed using his Force powers. The Jedi can fly many kinds of vehicles, including flying cars called airspeeders. Once, Obi-Wan piloted an underwater ship called a bongo!

Anakin uses all his Jedi skills to fly an airspeeder through a busy city.

Obi-Wan pilots his Jedi starfighter away from danger.

When the Jedi go on missions, they often fly small ships called starfighters. There is just enough space for the Jedi pilot and a small droid.

Pilot Droids
Pilot droids sit in spaceships with Jedi and help them to reach their destination. This droid is called R2-D2.

Space Battle

During the war in the galaxy, Jedi flew small attack ships called Interceptors. They are faster than ordinary starfighters. During a crucial space battle of the war, hundreds of spaceships fought each other. Anakin made many brave attacks in his Interceptor.

Obi-Wan flew close by Anakin in his own ship. Obi-Wan's ship was hit by enemy fire. Although he was in great danger, he managed to land his ship and get out just in time!

Anakin and Obi-Wan fly into the heart of the space battle.

Dark Side

The worst thing a Jedi can do is to turn away from the good side of the Force and begin using the dark side. One of the most powerful Jedi of all, Anakin Skywalker, turned to the dark side during the war. The evil Sith Lord Sidious persuaded Anakin to join him and become a Sith.

Anakin turned away from his loving wife, Padmé, and attacked the Jedi Temple. He killed many Jedi. Anakin even tried to kill his oldest friend and teacher, Obi-Wan. Obi-Wan did not want to fight his old friend, but he had no choice. It took all his strength and powers, but in end he thought he had killed Anakin. He was wrong.

A New Era

The war was the most dangerous time the galaxy had ever seen. Millions of people died, including nearly all of the Jedi. The evil Sith Lords won the war and ruled the galaxy. Anakin also survived and ruled alongside Emperor Palpatine. Now he was called Darth Vader and he wore a black helmet.

Darth Vader has the body of Anakin Skywalker, but he has turned to the dark side of the Force.

Luke Skywalker never thought he would become a Jedi, but he did.

A few Jedi survived. They hid until the time was right to destroy the Sith. They were led by Anakin's children, Luke and Leia. After many long battles, the Sith were destroyed.

As long as there are Jedi, there is hope for the galaxy. May the Force be with you!

Luke Skywalker is the son of Anakin and Padmé.

Glossary

Airspeeder
A type of flying car.

Apprentice
A person who is
learning a skill.

Blaster
A gun that fires a
deadly beam of light.

Comlink
A communication
device that sends and
receives messages.

Dark side
The part of the Force
associated with fear
and hatred.

Droid
A kind of robot.
R2-D2 is a droid.

Empire
A group of nations
ruled over by one
leader, who is called
an Emperor. Palpatine
is the Emperor who
rules the Galactic
Empire.

The Force
An energy field
created by all
living things.

Galactic
Something from or to
do with a galaxy.

Galaxy
A group of millions of
stars and planets.

Holoprojector
A device that records
still or moving images.

Interceptors
A type of Jedi attack
ship that is faster than
a starfighter.

Jedi Knight
A *Star Wars* warrior
with special powers
who defends the good
of the galaxy. Anakin
Skywalker, Luke
Skywalker, and
Ob-Wan Kenobi are
all Jedi Knights.

Jedi Master
The most experienced
Jedi of all.

Jedi Order
The name of a group
that defends peace
and justice in the
galaxy.

Jedi Temple
The Jedi headquarters
where the Jedi Council
meets and Jedi live,
train, and work.

Lightsaber
A Jedi's and Sith's
weapon, made of

glowing energy.

Light side
The part of the Force
associated with
goodness, compassion
and healing

Macrobinoculars
Binoculars that
electronically zoom in
on objects far away,
even in the dark.

Missions
Special tasks or duties.

Padawan Learner
A Jedi who is learning
the ways of the Force.

Republic
A nation or group of
nations in which the
people vote for their
leaders.

Sith
Enemies of the Jedi
who use the dark side
of the Force.

Starfighter
A small, fast spaceship
used by Jedi and
others.

Youngling
The first stage of Jedi
training, before you
become a Padawan
Learner.